Stress Test

S. harris

RUTGERS UNIVERSITY PRESS
New Brunswick, New Jersey

STRESS TEST

Cartoons on Medicine
Sidney Harris

All the cartoons in this book have been previously published and copyrighted by the following publications: *American Scientist, Chicago, Clinical Chemistry News, Datamation, Harvard Business Review, Hippocrates, Johns Hopkins Magazine, Medical Economics, Medical Tribune, National Lampoon, Phi Delta Kappan, Playboy, Practical Psychology, Punch, Science, The New Yorker, Today's Chemist, U.S. Medicine, Washingtonian,* and *Writer's Digest.*

Library of Congress Cataloging-in-Publication Data

Harris, Sidney.
   Stress test : cartoons on medicine / Sidney Harris.
      p. cm.
   ISBN 0-8135-2065-7 (pbk.)
   1. Medicine—Caricatures and cartoons.
2. American wit and humor. Pictorial. I. Title.
NC1429.H33315A4 1994
616'.00207—dc20   93-31590
                                    CIP

British Cataloging-in-Publication information available

To the memory of Shen Nung (ca. 2800 B.C.),
who tested 365 drugs on himself

Stress Test

"LET'S SEE NOW..."

1

"VERY WELL, I'LL INTRODUCE YOU. EGO, MEET ID. NOW GET BACK TO WORK."

3

"BELIEVE ON THE LORD, TAKE AN ANALGESIC FOR RELIEF OF PAIN AND MUSCLE SPASM, AN ANTI-DEPRESSANT TO REDUCE PSYCHIC TENSION, AND THROW AWAY YOUR CRUTCHES!"

4

"WHAT I REALLY HATE IS PREVENTIVE MEDICINE. THEY GO AFTER US BEFORE WE EVEN _DO_ ANYTHING."

"You can tell Dr. Ridley that I know Kleinzoff's Syndrome when I see it, and you don't have Kleinzoff's Syndrome."

7

8

"I'M LISTENING, ERSKINE, BUT THE DOCTOR
SAYS I'LL STAY CALMER IF I KEEP LOOKING
AT THE DAMN FISH."

"YES, WE'RE NOW THE LARGEST DRUG COMPANY IN THE COUNTRY."

"SORRY I'M LATE, BUT THAT'S WHY
I'M HERE. MY BIOLOGICAL CLOCK
IS ALL OUT OF WHACK."

11

"OF COURSE CONFIDENTIALITY IS VERY IMPORTANT, BUT WE HAVE TO BE TOLD WHAT THIS CASE IS ABOUT."

13

"I'M NOT INTERESTED, WE'RE FULLY MECHANIZED."

14

"I CAN UNDERSTAND MY MOTHER AND MY FIRST-GRADE TEACHER BEING THERE, BUT THERE'S ALSO A TV ANNOUNCER WHO DOES DOG FOOD COMMERCIALS AND A SECOND-STRING CATCHER FOR THE DETROIT TIGERS."

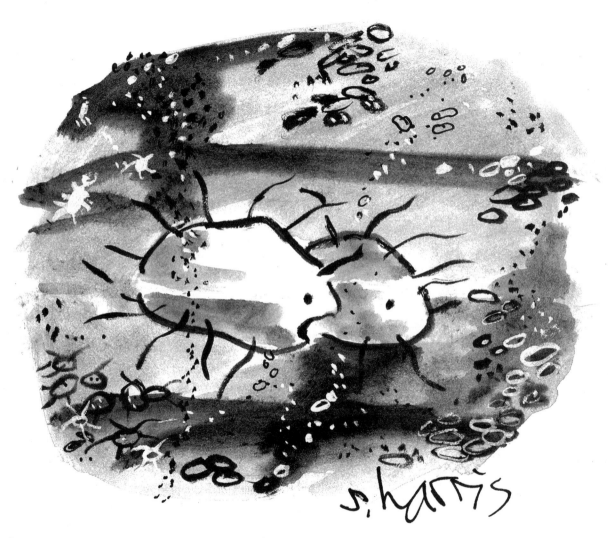

"YOU MEAN THIS SEWAGE HAS ALREADY BEEN TREATED?"

17

"I UTILIZE THE BEST FROM FREUD, THE BEST FROM JUNG AND THE BEST FROM MY UNCLE MARTY, A VERY SMART FELLOW."

18

LOUIS PASTEUR, AFTER DISCOVERING THAT MICROBES TRANSMIT DISEASE, EXPERIMENTED WITH METHODS FOR KILLING THEM

19

21

"TYPICAL 'TYPE A' BEHAVIOR."

22

"MY WIFE! THE MILKMAN! HELENE, HOW COULD YOU? YOU KNOW I HAVE LACTOSE INTOLERANCE,"

23

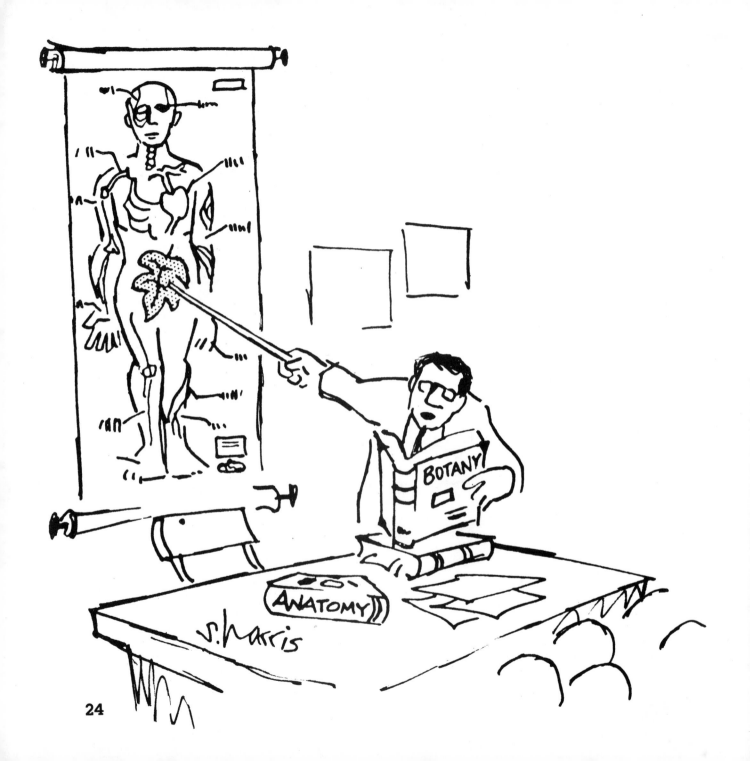

"THERE'S BEEN SOME SLIGHT MISTAKE HERE. YOU SHOULD HAVE BEEN SENT HOME ABOUT EIGHT MONTHS AGO." 25

"...AND TRY TO AVOID THE ENVIRONMENT FOR A COUPLE OF WEEKS."

HIPPOCRATES
FATHER OF
MEDICINE

ENDROCAS
FATHER OF
DENTISTRY

PHINILIAS
FATHER OF
UPWARD SPIRAL
OF HEALTH-CARE
COSTS

29

"YOU WON'T BELIEVE THIS, BUT EVEN IF THE VACCINE WORKS, THEY WON'T GIVE IT TO OTHER SICK MICE."

"OF COURSE IT TASTES LIKE CHICKEN SOUP. IT IS CHICKEN SOUP."

33

"I HAVEN'T HAD A MINUTE TO MYSELF RECENTLY.
I'M ON ONE COMMITTEE WHICH IS TRYING TO DETERMINE
WHEN HUMAN LIFE BEGINS, ANOTHER COMMITTEE SEARCHING
FOR THE <u>MEANING</u> OF LIFE, AND A THIRD COMMITTEE WHICH IS
TRYING TO DETERMINE WHEN LIFE IS LEGALLY OVER." 35

"FEWER THAN ONE IN TEN THOUSAND — SOMETHING LIKE ONE IN FOURTEEN THOUSAND — GETS THESE SIDE EFFECTS. HARDLY ANYBODY GETS THESE SIDE EFFECTS. THEY'RE EXTREMELY RARE. YOU SHOULD BE VERY PROUD."

37

"AN UNDERSTUDY HAS BECOME ILL, IS THERE
A MEDICAL STUDENT IN THE HOUSE?"

38

39

HERETOFORE UNNOTICED RESEMBLANCE
BETWEEN
G. WASHINGTON AND A. LINCOLN

"FORGET INFORMED CONSENT. JUST GIVE US YOUR UNINFORMED CONSENT."

41

"BUT YOU MUST ADMIT HALLUCINATIONS ARE MORE <u>INTERESTING</u> THAN DEPRESSION."

"WHAT WE'RE HOPING FOR ARE SOME MAJOR BREAKTHROUGHS WHICH WILL BE A BOON TO MANKIND AND WILL PROVIDE OUR STOCKHOLDERS WITH A SUBSTANTIAL RETURN ON THEIR INVESTMENTS."

43

"I'VE BECOME RESISTANT TO ALL ANTIBIOTICS, BUT WHAT I DREAD IS A SHOT OF WHISKY IN A CUP OF HOT TEA."

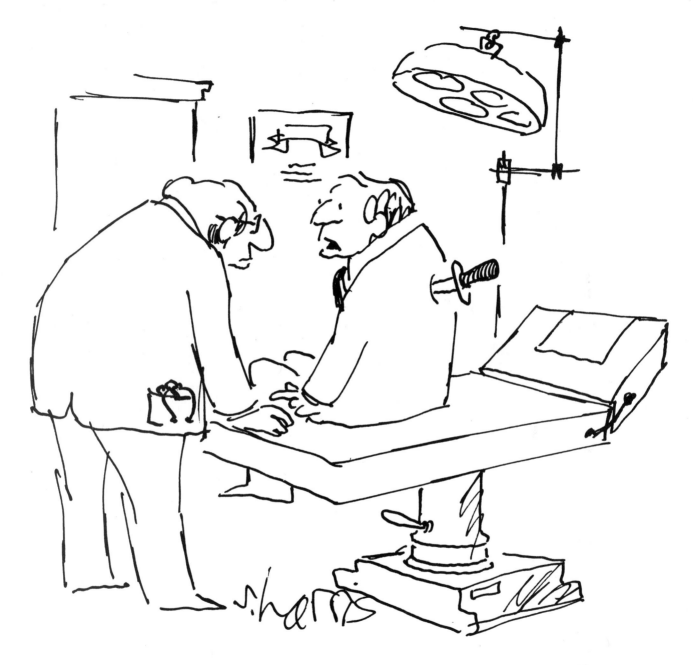

"I THINK I'D LIKE A SECOND OPINION." 47

"THAT'S THE SECOND TIME TODAY HE'S CROSSED THE THIN LINE BETWEEN GENIUS AND INSANITY."

"AT THAT POINT THE MEETING BECAME CHAOTIC, AS EVERYONE'S MEDICATION SEEMED TO WEAR OFF AT THE SAME TIME."

"YOUR FLAG HAS ONLY ELEVEN STRIPES."

"THAT'S AN AWFULLY LARGE SMALL INTESTINE
52 AND AN AWFULLY SMALL LARGE INTESTINE."

"IT TURNS OUT THAT THE DRUG WHICH WE THOUGHT WAS PATIENT-FRIENDLY IS REALLY VIRUS FRIENDLY."

"THINK BACK. WERE THERE ANY MUSICIANS IN THE ROOM WHEN WE OPERATED ON HIM?"

"ALL RIGHT—WHERE'S THE EPIDEMIC?"

..and...I'd like to be taken back... to Slovenia... and go by donkey cart... to the outskirts of Jindrichur Hradzek... on the far side of the river... up the hill... and be buried... in the family plot.

HE SAID HE'D LIKE TO BE CREMATED

v. harris

"FIND OUT WHO SET UP THIS EXPERIMENT. IT SEEMS THAT HALF OF THE PATIENTS WERE GIVEN A PLACEBO, AND THE OTHER HALF WERE GIVEN A DIFFERENT PLACEBO."

"JUST BECAUSE WE GOT FLEAS, THE FLEAS GOT LICE AND THE LICE GOT GERMS, WE GET BLAMED FOR SPREADING DISEASE."

EMERGENCY
ROOM
—
ADMITTING

S. Harris

"WE JUST DON'T GET INVOLVED WITH THINGS LIKE DOUBLE-BLIND TESTS AND PEER REVIEW. WE'RE JUST A LITTLE MOM-AND-POP LABORATORY."

"NOW, OF THE TWELVE DRUGS WE'VE TESTED ON YOU, WHICH ONE TASTED BEST?"

66

"OF COURSE I'M SURE IT'S HEREDITARY. MY FATHER TREATED YOUR FATHER FOR THE SAME 68 THING."

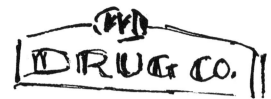

DRUG CO.

DEPT.	FL.
ADVERSE REACTIONS	3
CONTRAINDICATIONS	2
DOSAGE	1
INDICATIONS	1
OVERDOSAGE	3
PRECAUTIONS	2
USAGE	1
WARNINGS	2

S. Harris

"AMAZING — YOU HAVE THE HEART OF A 375-YEAR-OLD MAN."

Diet of a Track Star

BREAKFAST

Juice, oatmeal, skim milk

LUNCH

Broiled fish, baked potato, mixed vegetables, water

DINNER

Broiled chicken, rice, salad, juice

SNACKS

Hamburgers, hot dogs, ice cream, pie, cake, chips, beer

If I can't get through to your conscience, let's see how you respond to some low-back pain.

S. Harris

"MY APPROACH TO PSYCHIATRY IS THAT ALL THESE PROBLEMS ARE CAUSED BY VIRUSES." 75

"I DIDN'T EVEN KNOW HE WAS SICK."

"MY POLICY COVERS A COUPLE OF ASPIRIN, SOME BAND-AIDS AND A HOT-WATER BOTTLE. IT'S CALLED 'MINOR MEDICAL.'"

MING DYNASTY ACUPUNCTURE CHART
78 (DISTRIBUTED BY MING DYNASTY BANDAGE CO.)

MICROSURGERY

"REMEMBER THIS, RADKIN — I'VE GOT A DISEASE NAMED AFTER ME; YOU'VE ONLY GOT A SYNDROME."

81

HYPOCHONDRIA
HOSPITAL

S.harris

82

83

"30% OF EVERYTHING IS A PLACEBO. THE OTHER 70% MAKES THINGS WORSE."

"TAKE SOME INTERFERON, AND CALL ME IN THE MORNING."

"RUN FOR THE HILLS! THE RECOMBINANT DNA HAS ESCAPED!"

87

"IT ONLY HURTS WHEN I THROW
A HIGH, INSIDE CURVE."

"SURE WE'RE LOOKING FOR A SUBSTANCE TO
CHANGE LEAD INTO GOLD, AND A SUBSTANCE TO
PROLONG LIFE INDEFINITELY, BUT IT DOESN'T
HAVE TO BE THE SAME SUBSTANCE."

"FORGET FREUD. THOREAU IS THE ANSWER. WORK IN YOUR GARDEN. EAT BEANS AND SQUASH. WRITE ABOUT IT."

"WHAT BURNS ME UP IS I WORK AS HARD AS I CAN, AND THEY CALL ME A 'LOW-GRADE' INFECTION."

"I WAS DRIVING ALONG, TALKING ON MY CELLULAR PHONE, WHEN SUDDENLY MY OTHER CELLULAR PHONE RANG."

"WHAT DO YOU MEAN 'DON'T EXPECT MIRACLES'? WHY SHOULDN'T I EXPECT MIRACLES?"

93

...and the pollen count is 126 today.

s.harris

FLORENCE NIGHTINGALE, THE CRIMEAN WAR'S LADY OF THE LAMP, ABOUT TO BURN DOWN ANOTHER MILITARY HOSPITAL

95

"IT'S JUST A MILD HYPERINSULISM DUE TO ISLET CELL HYPERPLASIA WITH A TOUCH OF HEPATIC INSUFFICIENCY AND GLYCOGEN DEPLETION. IN OTHER WORDS, WATCH YOUR DIET."

97

"I THOUGHT THEY'D HIT IT OFF. THEY'RE ALL GOING THROUGH THEIR MID-LIFE CRISES."

"BUT IT WOULDN'T BE EASY TO GET EVERYONE TO WEAR THAT ALL THE TIME."

"DR. KT-26 WILL NOW INSTALL THE ARTIFICIAL HEART."

"THE AIR TODAY IS SMOOTHER TO THE TOUCH,
102 BUT IT DOESN'T TASTE VERY GOOD."

"I SEE YOUR INSURANCE COVERS LITTLE GREEN PILLS, LITTLE YELLOW PILLS, LITTLE WHITE PILLS, LITTLE RED PILLS AND LITTLE PURPLE PILLS, WHAT I'M GOING TO GIVE YOU ARE SOME LITTLE BLUE PILLS."

"IT DOESN'T MATTER HOW YOU FEEL. IT'S A MATTER OF DEFINITION, AND ACCORDING TO THE LATEST, YOU'RE LEGALLY DEAD."

"I'M GLAD YOU CAME TO ME. VISIONS OF GHOSTS OF CHRISTMAS PAST, PRESENT AND FUTURE ARE CLEARLY DELUSIONS BASED ON UNDERLYING PSYCHOLOGICAL CONFLICTS."

"I FEEL BETTER TODAY TOO, BUT AROUND HERE I'VE LEARNED NOT TO BE TOO OPTIMISTIC."

"THEY'RE ALL GOOD, BUT I PREFER **AB NEGATIVE.**"

"GOLF! GOLF! DOCTOR, YOU DON'T UNDERSTAND. GOLF IS WHAT'S <u>MAKING</u> ME A NERVOUS WRECK."

"I CAN'T TELL IF THE DOCTOR WROTE 'FURONUT' OR 'FORUNONIL' OR 'FERNOBIL,' SO I'M GIVING YOU A LITTLE OF EACH."

"EAT A STEAK. THERE ARE SO MANY ANTIBIOTICS IN IT, YOU'LL BE CURED." 111

"IT DOESN'T LOOK TO ME LIKE IT COULD DO ANY CHROMOSOMAL DAMAGE."

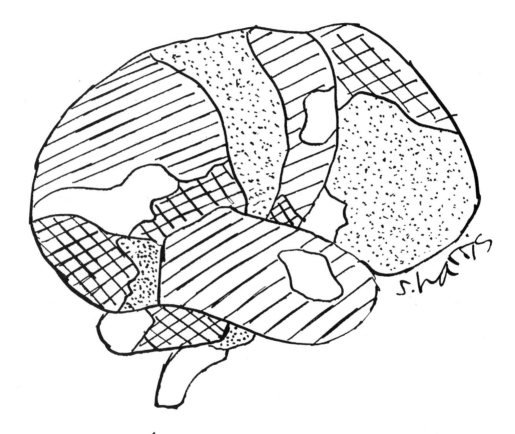

NORMAL BRAIN

☐ ACTIVE
▨ DOZING
▩ ASLEEP
⬚ DISTRACTED

113

"THE RESULT OF ALL THIS IS THAT THE MEDICAL CENTER WANTS ME TO LEAVE THEM MY BRAIN."

"I THINK...YES...HIS NAME IS HERE ON THE DOOR: A. VAN LEEUWENHOEK."

"THERE COULD BE ANY NUMBER OF CAUSES FOR THIS CONDITION. PERHAPS HE BROKE A MIRROR OR WALKED UNDER A LADDER OR SPILLED SOME SALT..."

"THAT'S THE PROBLEM. EVEN THOUGH IT'S RECOMBINANT, WE CAN'T MAKE IT DECOMBINANT."

"THE FOOD AND DRUG ADMINISTRATION IS REALLY CRACKING DOWN. NOW WE HAVE TO LIST ALL THE INGREDIENTS IN OUR POTIONS."

119

"WELL YOU CAN GO BACK TO DR. KENDRICK AND TELL HIM THAT I SAID YOUR BROKEN ARM HAS AN ORGANIC CAUSE."

"I KNOW YOU HAVE GOOD INTENTIONS, BUT YOU'LL NEED LOTS AND LOTS OF HELP. YOU JUST CAN'T START AN EPIDEMIC BY YOURSELF."

"I'D SAY THE SALES CHART IS THE ULCER, THE PHONE IS THE HYPERTENSION, THE PAPERWORK IS THE MIGRAINE..."

"THIS PLAY IS BASED ON THE HOPE THAT ALL THEIR TRICK KNEES WILL GIVE OUT AT ONCE."

123

124 "MY COMPLIMENTS TO THE FOOD TASTER."

"ANYONE HERE WHO DIDN'T TAKE THE HIPPOCRATIC OATH?"

126 "NEVER MIND YOUR VOW OF SILENCE—
SAY 'AH.'"

"YOU'RE SUFFERING FROM AN OVERDOSE OF VITAMIN C. I'M GOING TO GIVE YOU SOME COMMON COLD VIRUS TO COMBAT IT."

"Don't forget, this medicine worked better on the rat than it did on the guinea pig, and I think he's more like a guinea pig."

"SURE, I'M QUALIFIED. I STUDIED ALL THE NORMAL SUBJECTS: LAYING ON OF HANDS, MIRACLES, TALKING IN TONGUES..."

"I CAN REFER YOU TO DR. BASINSKI, A NOTED SPECIALIST, DR. HODGE-CABOT, A PIONEER IN THE FIELD, OR CHARLIE, A GENERIC DOCTOR WHO ALSO DOES A VERY GOOD JOB."

"I'LL HAVE TO GET DR. CURTIS TO REDUCE
132 HIS DOSAGE OF THE MOOD-ELEVATOR."

"EVER HAVE ONE OF THOSE GREAT DAYS WHEN YOU'RE JUST BETWEEN MANIC AND DEPRESSIVE?"

133

"A GOOD THROW BY CAMPBELL, WHO IS IN A DRUG-REHABILITATION PROGRAM, AND IT'S CAUGHT BY SANCHEZ AT FIRST BASE, WHO HASN'T HAD A DRINK IN SIX WEEKS."

"It's simple. Your frantic travel schedule and compulsive gift giving are merely your way of compensating for the fact that you don't have any children of your own."

"THEY'RE USING US TO TEST A DRUG FOR GUINEA PIGS, AND THEY'RE USING GUINEA PIGS TO TEST A DRUG FOR US."

"THESE CAPSULES ARE NOT JUST ANOTHER CHEMICAL THERAPY FOR A PERSONALITY DISTURBANCE. EACH ONE CONTAINS A MINIATURE TRANSISTOR SYSTEM THAT, THROUGHOUT THE DAY, WILL ANNOUNCE POSITIVE AND UPLIFTING IDEAS TO YOU."

137

"ON THE CONTRARY, I CAN'T RECALL A THING FROM FIFTY YEARS AGO, BUT I REMEMBER EXACTLY WHAT I HAD FOR LUNCH YESTERDAY."

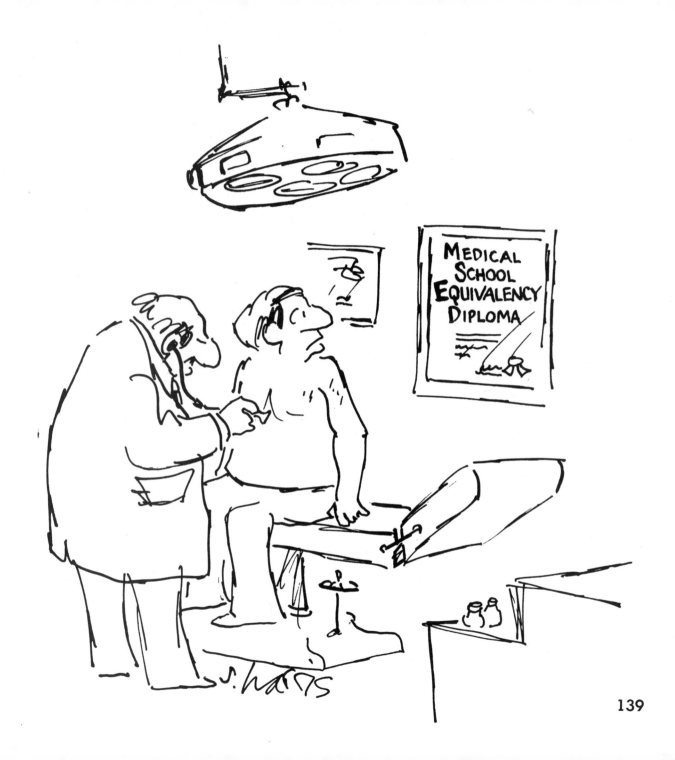

MEDICAL
SCHOOL
EQUIVALENCY
DIPLOMA

139

"DON'T PANIC. I'M JUST A SORE THROAT."

"WE'VE RUN THE WHOLE GAMUT OF TESTS ON YOU, AND YOU NOW APPEAR TO BE SUFFERING FROM OVERTESTING."

"IF ONLY THERE WERE SOME PEACEFUL
142 USES FOR NERVE GAS."

"NEVER HAVE THERE BEEN SO MANY OPPORTUNITIES FOR OUR GRADUATES... RESEARCH, GENETIC ENGINEERING, MEDICAL PHYSICS... AND, I HOPE, SOME OF YOU ACTUALLY PRACTICING MEDICINE."

"WHO SAID 'OOPS!'?"

"I CAN REMEMBER WHEN PARANOIA WAS UNUSUAL."

145

"MEGAVITAMIN THERAPY—THAT'S THE ANSWER."

"I GIVE UP. WHERE'S THE PATIENT?"

147

"HOW ABOUT: 'THE SURGEON GENERAL HAS DETERMINED THAT MARIJUANA MAY OR MAY NOT BE DANGEROUS TO YOUR HEALTH, DEPENDING ON WHICH AUTHORITIES YOU BELIEVE'?"

"WELL, MY LAWYER SAYS I HAVE TO CHECK YOUR BLOOD PRESSURE."

"IF YOU ASK ME, THESE EXPENSIVE
FUNERALS ARE BECOMING ONE BIG RACKET."